Bly & Loveland Press
5537 Zenith Avenue South
Edina, MN 55410
loveland@mlecmn.net
www.blyandloveland.com

Library of Congress Control Number: 2006901603
ISBN: 0-9745000-3-8

Front cover painting:
Seascape, Corbière by Herbert Barnard John Everett
BHC0023
With permission of:
©National Maritime Museum
Greenwich, London

Printed in the United States of America by
Metro Printing
Eden Prairie, MN

Designed by
DeeAnn Hendricks

Against Workshopping Manuscripts
Copyright © Bly & Loveland Press 2006
All rights reserved, including rights to reproduce this book
or portions thereof in any form whatsoever.

Set in ITC Garamond Std type

Footnotes appear on the pages of their referent text. We have provided quoted passages in closed font so that they can be located easily.

Please send all orders and inquiries to:
Bly & Loveland Press
5537 Zenith Avenue South
Edina, MN 55410

$20

Against Workshopping Manuscripts

A Plea for Justice to Student Writers

By Carol Bly and Cynthia Loveland

This book is dedicated to writers in MFA programs and summer writers' conferences.

They trust their teachers to help them wake up their own minds.

They trust MFA programs to model how to teach *others* to wake up *their* minds.

Both they and their teachers hope that the cash-cow style of creative-writing workshopping hasn't gone so far that it can't be cleaned up.

A Table of Contents

Five ways to replace the workshopping of manuscripts	9
What exactly *is* "workshopping a manuscript?"	11
Some history of manuscript workshopping	13
The *real* vs the "good" reason for English departments' having so universally taken to workshopping manuscripts	16
General psychological damage done by workshopping manuscripts	18
Harm specific to children caused by putting them into small creative-writing groups	26
Psychological harm done youth by middle- and high-school workshopping groups	28
Suppression of the imagination aggravated by the workshopping of manuscripts	29
The practice of workshopping manuscripts seen as a toxic environment for re-entry in the neocortex because workshopping obviates empathic inquiry	31

An Appendix

Neurologists of interest about cortical pathways of the imagination	37
A general bibliography	39
Great literature for writers	41
Two prescient passages of William Wordsworth on imagination	45
Empathic inquiry for writers only	47
About the authors—Carol Bly and Cynthia Loveland	51

Carol Bly and Cynthia Loveland

Five Ways to Replace the Workshopping of Manuscripts

1. No creative-writing class should have more than 15 participants.

2. All creative-writing instructors in any venue should specifically learn how to do *empathic inquiry* so they can, in turn, teach writers the long, middle (second) stage of writing a manuscript of any kind. Without any knowledge of specific empathic inquiry, teachers can teach the *first* stage of manuscript development, which is inspiration or mere jotting or a mix of the two. Without any knowledge of specific empathic inquiry they can teach the *third* stage, which is making literary fixes. They cannot do much with the middle stage, however. Most instructors, in fact, make a dog's breakfast out of that part of the writing process that involves *deepening one's first idea*.

3. In creative work, as opposed to scholarly essays, no rough drafts should ever be asked for. Until writers have got through the psychological, middle stage of working up a piece of writing, they cannot and should not be trying to plan how the work will end. Assigning rough drafts cuts off the psychological privacy in which the deepest, happiest, saddest, most charged potential of stories and poems still crouch profoundly hidden in the writers' thickets of neurons.

4. Writing students should be asked to hand in many short works during any writing course so that their teachers regularly read one- or two-page examples of their work and comment on it mid-course. Why? So that students trust themselves to re-imagine their own argument or narrative.

Another reason: a sad aspect of conventional American culture is that both experienced and inexperienced teachers have trouble believing that the human mind inside any unpromising-sounding student writer may well be capable of and longing to write with philosophical beauty. Thomas Grey had it right: the annals of unprivileged people's lives are short and simple because more privileged people (for which *legitur* "teachers") don't expect much of the gum-chewers and yawners in their writing workshops.

About these unpromising student writers, whose short and simple annals are so unpromising not to mention misspelled: how *would* they ever discover any complex and numinous feelings inside themselves? Which was the day-care staffer with orders and time to praise each little kid who said something original? Which is the public high-school teacher of 5 crowded classes who even begins to read 150 papers over each weekend? How many parents, doing their best by their children, protecting them from random molesting as they go off to school, know how to praise *originality* when one or another of their children show it?

A creative-writing teacher has the best chance to sight some students' ingenuity if writing is handed in frequently. And such recognition of one's own beauty of feeling or thought by a writing teacher can buoy up writers who haven't ever moved among people who appreciate original language or fresh story plot. Thousands of beginning writers take themselves for "just average, they guess." No one has ever shown them that in the *H.sapiens* neocortex there is no average.

5. Finally, no student nor teacher nor other colleague in a group of writers should monkey with literary fixing, the third stage of any work on a piece of literature, until all the inward deepest feelings of the material have found their home-away-from-home—namely, when they have leapt from the writer's brain like live creatures onto the page.

What Exactly *Is* "Workshopping a Manuscript?"

Workshopping manuscripts means that writers in a class make one copy apiece for their facilitator or teacher and each fellow-student.

On a scheduled day the class meets to discuss a certain student's manuscript. Everyone has read it, honorably, carefully, or hastily, skimming, or heedless of the author's intent or not.

The writer is to sit silent while the others take it in turns to offer their suggestions.

Such hot-seat style has two curious aspects to it. First, it stops authors from wasting group time defending themselves. Second, it is a perfect opening for drawing-room irony. If class members aren't conscious of the psychological pull of drawing-room irony they slide into indulging in it. Example: if the author has expressed vulnerable and deep feeling, a fellow-class member knows better than to grin and squeal "Give me a Break! You felt what! Have I got this right? You really felt 'mortally touched'? Please give me a break!" No one will say that. Instead they may exercise drawing-room irony. They give credence and mild praise to technical aspects of whatever the passage with "mortally touched" in it. Then they give light smiles of approval, if any response at all, to the issue of being mortally touched. The light smiles are the smiles that atheist parents give to their children's nightly prayers. Somehow the hot-seated author is not deceived. He or she feels such an ass.

When I was a visiting author to a graduate writing course at Syracuse University, I experienced my first formal "workshopping of a manuscript." Like the others, I had read the manuscript in advance. The writer sat silent at our table. As the others made their comments in turn, the author remained silent. When it was my turn, I asked the writer questions in the common mode of teachers who use empathic questioning. The student now glistened with sweat. Still, he did not answer. At last the course professor explained the workshopping rules to me. The student was not allowed to answer.

I was appalled at the practice. The practice of silence, however, is held dear as a part of the workshopping format. Its specs preclude any empathic inquiry that could be made to the author by a fellow student because empathy requires both cordial questions and equable answers—namely, intelligent exchange.

Each member of a graduate-level writing workshop has paid between $1500 and $3000 to take such a course. In return for that outlay they have to teach each other with whatever ideas they may have. Hours of reading fellow students' manuscripts! Hours of trying to comment on them when you yourself are only a beginning writer! No wonder people complain of the elementary level of literary technique endlessly, repetitively, put forth.

We have permission to quote a heart-breaking letter.

> "My name is Clint Barker, an English education major from St. Olaf College. During the tail part of my last semester as well as over this summer, I have been reading—and rereading—your book *Beyond the Writers' Workshop*. The subject line is not facetious. It saved my career in education.
>
> I have had only one writing class either in high school or in college, and it used the workshop almost entirely. I did enjoy this class, but not because of the pedagogy. The professor was witty,

entertaining and informative. Unfortunately, most of the class time had nothing to do with interaction with the professor. The class time was spent mostly giving and receiving comments (mostly the same comments over and over) in the manner that I now know, thanks to your book, is identical to that of most other workshops. I finished that semester liking the class, liking the professor, but having absolutely no more writing skills than when I went in."[1]

Some History of Manuscript-Workshopping

As with the gradual establishment of any bad practice, complaints are few at first. Americans tend to feel diffident about any novel pedagogy that is an immediate commercial success. They suppose they should have thought it up themselves. Participants in the Iowa Workshop complained much more of the ugliness of seeing their manuscripts in purple ditto than of anything like psychological stunting. Of course there were whistleblowers from the beginning. In the middle of the decade of the 1950s, however, nobody paid respectful attention to whistleblowers against workshopping, because at the time workshops were conducted in noisy, male-dominated, jaunty, and very boisterous settings. Males in them had served in World War II and barrack life is always conducted in a noisy, male-dominated style of jeering and kidding. It seemed normal. In the 1950s the women's movement had not gathered critical mass to point out jeering is not just normal, but normal *and unethical*. Wit that hurts sounded O.K. to sometime corporals and sergeants, especially if they hadn't read Mr Knightley's heavy scolding of Emma for bullying Mrs and Miss Bates.

With respect to workshopping manuscripts, intelligent critics as early as the1950s remarked on the tamped-down, neutral gravel of so many of the poetry manuscripts issuing from Paul

---

[1] Clint Barker, St Olaf College, September 8, 2005.

Engle's Iowa Workshop. But still, the ingenuity of the idea! Dispatching a group to do what had been the labor-intensive work of instructor and student one-on-one! Ingenious!

Later, poetry publishers joked about scorning manuscripts postmarked Iowa City and Cedar Rapids.

As the next stage of workshopping developed, luck stepped in. Enough imitators, with notably lower standards than the original, cropped up in universities so that the original Iowa Workshop itself glittered in contrast.

At last, as in any business enterprise, everyone could discern a *range* of quality and non-quality performance. America is a huge country. Its population since 1950 has geometrically increased. We have thousands and thousands of "creative writers." The best try for the now hallowed Iowa Workshop, and by increments, those of lesser skill get served by lesser schools. All the way down to summer writing conferences a good many of whose teachers write scarcely any literature themselves. Modern phenomena in creative writing include low-residency writing colleges, and high-residency prisons with inmate writing groups. Some good, some deprived of imaginative leadership.

Once people are so inured to a practice that their concern is only to buy the best they can win entrance to, it is hard to change the question from *Which is the best?* to *Should I be doing this at all?*

Workshopping of manuscripts has huge critical mass. It profits hugely in its dependence on heavy networking. Blurbs for books must come from somewhere. Recommendations for assistant-professorships or at least one- and three-year appointments to teaching programs must come from somewhere. Since other college English departments or Creative-Writing programs teach creative writing, so, deans and presidents took to thinking, so must we. Personal-fulfillment courses have always been handsome cash cows. Now, more and more, MFA programs are taking bites out of their market.

A piece of sociology is a factor: the intellectual penury of elementary and high-school English pedagogy is showing up in young people who soon fail in the publishing internships they attempt. More people can't make it through graduate programs in Business Administration. Universities and colleges themselves have madly lowered their entrance requirements and inflated grades given, but what shall they do about people who need post-graduate degrees?

A canny university needs a Flunk-Out U graduate program. If we will sign up for and take this Flunk-Out U kind of program, the institution in turn will grease the ways for us. What program for a master's degree of some sort can we get into that won't make the college or university itself a laughing-stock? —yet at the same time promises the student he or she will pass the course? The perfect answer? Creative Writing. Who can tell if a Creative Writing program is or is not letting incompetent students receive higher degrees? Even though MFA programs are known for both unclear entrance requirements and automatic high grading, no one can point to some idiot who got through with the same ease that people identify idiots who hold the MBA degree.

All this to draw attention to the fact that administration, its people being pressured by still higher-ups, influences how truly or how untruly an MFA writers' workshop student is served. Faculty members may not even have a choice in how many students get jammed into one classroom with others. Faculty members, then, with huge classes, may not have the choice of stopping workshopping manuscripts.

Our book complains of workshopping manuscripts, but unlike some critics who blame workshopping for the overwhelming mediocrity of current American literature, we don't.

That mediocrity comes of the following:

Writers' having been raised by parents who did not read aloud.

Writers' being dumped into day care where reading aloud follows the routine practice of asking children to tie the story to *something in their own lives*. This obviates their learning to use their imaginations to empathize with *other* for the very reason that it is other.

Writers' being pushed to market to a dumbed-down culture where sex and violence and fast paced action is valued. The writer is encouraged to write for audience rather than to write for oneself.

Mediocrity comes of adults', young people's, and children's watching of television hours each day even when they have decided to be contemplative or intelligent people. Television prevents anyone from retiring into one's own castle of the feelings—which means the brain doesn't get much practice in re-entry.[2]

To summarize about mediocrity: the widespread mediocrity in present student writing and impoverishment in language is not the fault of writers' workshops.

THE REAL VERSUS THE "GOOD" REASON[3] FOR ENGLISH DEPARTMENTS' HAVING SO UNIVERSALLY TAKEN TO WORKSHOPPING OF MANUSCRIPTS

The real reason that university English departments are so keen on the workshopping of manuscripts appears to be that workshopping demands so little from the instructors and professors.

---

[2] See the Appendix for a short bibliography of up-to-date neurological thinking. Re-entry will also be discussed later in this book.

[3] The essayist John Middleton Murry asked readers to differentiate between the "good" reasons they would give to anyone who asked, "Whyever did you do that?"—and the *real* reason they did it.

Since 2003 Bly & Loveland Press have several times challenged the ethicality of creative-writing teachers who teach by workshopping manuscripts.

A nasty revelation in the ensuing quarrels has been that more than once a writing professor, who has been energetically defending the workshopping of manuscripts on a principled level, suddenly exclaims late in the argument, "Anyway, I couldn't begin to teach the number of writing students I have unless they workshopped! I couldn't plan all those classes, not to mention the fact I would never have time to read all those papers!"

That is the copperhead curled in the road rut: time-saving for the teachers. Money-saving for a university determined to hire too few teachers for the job. In the scramble, teachers clip the students in order to appear competent getting through the required work of their own jobs. The students, either with good will or with scorn, cover for them. After all, those teachers will or will not write recommendations for them.

That is corruption of a conventional kind. Like all corruption it thrives if everybody's doing it and everyone accepts the understood lie—that is, that no harm is done. We must all agree that denying writers private mentoring over manuscripts does no harm. We must all agree not to bring out in public how much less work we are doing than our students had hoped of us. How empty creative-writing syllabi can be!—because most of the time was spent not on syllabus heads but on workshopping the group's manuscripts.

Workshopping of manuscripts is a pedagogical issue something like the issue of encouraging student writers to lie in memoirs for the sake of literary charm or adding pizzazz. If institutions don't make a stand against such lying, it will continue despite spates of *New York Times* and other coverage on this issue in January, 2006.

If institutions don't stand up against the workshopping of manuscripts in creative-writing programs, workshopping will continue. It is a tremendous gift of leisure to the teachers. It is a tremendous gift to whoever finances the university. They may keep core-faculty appointments to a minimum yet fill their student quota. To make this clear: if it were stopped, and teacher and writer spent hours in critiquing and questioning one another, *that* would be a tremendous gift to the students in creative-writing programs.

At the moment, most American writing students are habituated to workshopping. It is even, surrealistically, advertised to them in some college English departments, as the new "good pedagogy" as opposed to "the old way." Normalization of shabby behavior by habit was an ancient psychological dynamic long before Alexander Pope said "Whatever is, is right."

GENERAL PSYCHOLOGICAL DAMAGE DONE BY WORKSHOPPING OF MANUSCRIPTS

When the mind knows its innermost ideas will be exposed to non-professional outsiders, the mind will screen back its keenest ideas in order to avoid contumely.

Alexis de Tocqueville noted in *Democracy in America* nearly two centuries ago that Americans tend to be intimidated by one another in any event.

Workshopping of creative-writing manuscripts lets our national proclivity for bullying flood into our private hearts. This isn't bullying in the middle of a football field. One can't try bucking up an intellectually insulted workshop student by crying, "Look! You signed up for football! You asked for it!"

People's minds obviously track ideas from the culture along with those building from within: a spirited-enough "small group" can make a writer, who has just, as they say, "shared" with the others, feel that only his or her most ordinary, most familiar ideas are good, and the others are merely bizarre.

Nowhere is the American strain of schmooze more devastating than in small groups of writers. The very normalness of it—the viscous politeness of it—stiffens its covert blows. We would be missing the power of it to say that pearls were being cast down before swine. They're not. Most people's thinking and writing are not pearls and very, very few members of writers' classes or conferences deliberately behave swinishly. The particular point here is this psychological truth: nearly everyone in any group will negatively reinforce any material they haven't heard before. They will negatively reinforce it because it seems to have no authority. It is simply some sort of un-i.d.ed object that has shown up in the landscape. Actually, uneducated people love ideas that they take to be authorized. A cliché is often greeted affectionately in simple communities: "How about them Steelers?" let's say. That has a lot more authority and therefore feels less threatening than "I thought the Steelers were extraordinary this afternoon."

A startling aspect of how ordinary people judge a remark or a manuscript: if it contains metaphors they have never heard before they won't exclaim to themselves, "Thank goodness someone is saying something fresh and new here!" They will feel uneasy. They will wonder, "What if this writer is crazy? I mean, this is just so different-sounding!"

Say that a first-year MFA student named William Butler Yeats puts a poem up to be workshopped. Well, there he is with the hair and all, the clothes so last year you couldn't believe—but wait, this writing group do schmooze, no outright meanness ever. Civility. Camaraderie. No overt jeering.

They listen to him. Then they take it in turns to comment. They smile deeply at Yeats and say they really liked how he wrote about an older fellow, the way he did, because older guys' stories need to be told, too, but if he would kind of not be so negative about the old guy being like "a paltry thing, a tattered coat upon a stick, unless soul clap its hands and sing," he might reach a wider audience.[4] Then, each in turn, they would follow the routine for how to manage when you have been ambivalent. They let their voices trail off. If you let your voice trail off, you are being modest. What's more, dodging under that modesty, you are making it possible to take back all the criticism you gave.

Please note, too, that the word "ambivalent" in 21st-century writers' workshops gets used to mean not ambivalent but *opposed*. It is trickier to run an intellectual bureaucracy than a business-based bureaucracy because you have to use words associated with intellectual discernment—words like "ambivalent." You also have to use expressions like "in context" even more than diplomats and business executives do because that phrase, "in context," implies having read up some background and distinguished one circumstance from another. What is harmful about such usages—"ambivalent" used to mean "on the other side" or "opposed" and "in context" used (as it is) to mean "not demonstrably true" is that the speaker is lying about his or her real feeling about the work under discussion.

The speaker doesn't like the work but will not say so. A decade or two of the American workshopping culture in which unfavorable remarks are indecorous have marked their creature.

In any group of creative-writing students at least two will have heard and believed that literature is written *with audience in mind*. In that same group very likely no one has read Wordsworth on how creativity moves from initial perception to concept—Wordsworth saying the mind doesn't stop at

---

[4] The lines are taken from the second stanza of "Sailing to Byzantium" by W.B. Yeats:
> An aged man is but a paltry thing,
> A tattered coat upon a stick, unless
> Soul clap its hands and sing, and louder sing
> For every tatter in its mortal dress"

examining only how a daffodil cheers it up. A mind, in full imagination, will enjoy little lambs gamboling only if it can get those sheep tied to our mortal dread of meaningless and death.[5]

Let's leave Wordsworth and listen to Yeats being workshopped. Someone has just opened his mouth and made this suggestion: "The poem will sell to wider market if you take out that crack about a senior being nothing but a tattered coat upon a stick and all."

Once a group hear a designated critic make public pronouncement like that they seldom object. Even if one or two if its members feel the public statement was reprehensible, they find it hard or impossible to interject justice. We have to bear in mind how very, very passive Americans are simply for lack of brave models. Not having read much literature they are chock full of what's normal—the guillotine, not Sidney Carton, for example. The cocktail-partying mother making ironical jokes over her daughter's prayers for another example.[6]

1990s and 2000s neuroscientists are now writing accessibly about how the neocortex of the human brain is constantly comparing notes from one neighborhood of thought to another, measuring the truth against startling new information or stimulus from the outside. We are grateful for this good news from the wonderful upper mantle of our brains, this neocortex. It spreads any news it gets through the senses all over and through the six layers of its chemical and fiery neuron groupings. Those neurons signal back and forth to one another. They adjust,

---

[5] The poem obliquely referred to here is Wordsworth's "Intimations of Immortality from Recollections of Early Childhood."
[6] If you have never read Jim Harrison's "The Woman Lit by Fireflies" you may never have heard any criticism of parents lightly kidding about their kids' religious feelings during the cocktail hour. What would make you speak up to stop a class critic from saying another class member's work needed better marketing when what someone should have praised was an interesting psychological idea in the work under discussion— namely (W. B. Yeats idea) that to live by high and noble feelings is what the old must set themselves to.

revise, object: they weigh old insights or memories against the new impressions. *Re-entry* is one of the words for their work. It is what William Wordsworth was describing in his "Preface to *Lyrical Ballads, 2nd Edition*, 1801.[7]

It is curious to see how fear of one's peers does not just make you an aesthetic dullard: it does psychological damage. When sights and issues are recalled in "tranquility," as Wordsworth puts it, the writer experiences an affectionate mix of moral and aesthetic growth. But what about if there is no "tranquility" to recall anything in? Here is the double-bindedness of this. When re-entry is not practiced, the human brain gets bored and longs for stimulus that it is not getting by exercising its own resources. It needs violence and sensation. It doesn't consciously know what it is missing. It simply acts jerkily and without confidence: it lurches toward violence. As Wordsworth lamented in the "sick German sensationalism" that he cited—writers then feed themselves on more and more cruel happenings and sensationalism.

Young American writers display a noticeable taste for sadism, partly, not entirely, for the sake of marketing. The writer recognizes that other young Americans (the targeted audience) love sadistic sensationalism, so they themselves feed the craving.

It shows up as a sideshow to the circus of recent literary lying. Nicole Helget's memoir, *The Summer of Ordinary Ways*[8], includes a scene in which the author says her father killed a cow by stabbing it with a pitchfork. The author reports abuse in the home: her family howled in objection. Their claim was that neither the pitchforking to death nor the family abuse took

---

[7] Please see the two extraordinarily prescient passages in the Appendix.
[8] Nicole Helget's publisher is Minnesota Historical Society Press, 2005. Bart Schneider, editor of *Speakeasy* magazine, which awarded Helget its Speakeasy Prize for the first chapter, took a benignant attitude about fudging or non-fudging of facts in it, when interviewed by Mary Ann Grossmann of the St Paul *Pioneer Press*.

place. The question has been, did or did not Nicole Helget lie in her memoir? The side question is very little discussed: why use lies expressly to juice up a manuscript with sadism?

This question was directly brought up by Ted Kooser in 1998. Kooser wrote an essay about a clean-cut situation of lying in order to add sadistic relish to poetry.[9] Kooser, not then Poet Laureate of the United States, expressed himself openly horrified that a young poet, the step-mother of her husband's child, would report that the child's mother had disfigured the child by cutting it in a drunken rage. Kooser asked her, he says, if it were true. She answered blithely that it was *not* true—that the child had been marked by an innocent accident—but then she said to him (and Kooser quoted her verbatim) "I just thought my version would make a better poem."

In this book we can't and won't take up the question of how a culture could have produced so many sensation-hungry people as it has done, willing to lie in order to upgrade the horror felt by readers.

Before reiterating an explanation of that repulsive yearning from either Wordsworth's insights or modern neuroscientific insights, we want to mention another *kind* of sadism common in American literature since the 1980s. That is this: many young writers feel constrained to produce for the emotional scenery in their work a repellent sexuality.

One must allow for their previous teachers' not admiring Peter Elbow's warning against writing for audience.[10] Usually, in fact, previous writing teachers have told them they *should* "consider the audience." Then it would follow, logically, that their audiences, being in large part American audiences, have

---

[9] Ted Kooser, "Lying for the Sake of Making Poems." *Prairie Schooner,* Spring 1998, page 5.
[10] Peter Elbow, "Closing My Eyes As I Speak: An argument for Ignoring Audience." *College English* 49, no. 1 (January 1987): 50.

been brought up on TV and without books so they crave cynicism and cruelty. Then I suppose it follows: one must provide cynicism and cruelty. Such a teacher leads his or her classes into the commercial herd naturally, the way teachers in graduate schools of business do what they must do: produce ethics dilemma conferences that are little to do with ethics and much to do with staying out of jail when your corporation is profitably engaged in illegal practice of some sort.[11]

This is not a new issue for professional school faculty. If Thracymachus or Glaucon[12] instead of Socrates had been running the Athens school they'd have behaved in a parallel way. That is, when you live in a time of empire as they then did and we now do, you are rightly afraid of groups. In republics individuals have much more say than in empires where huge groups run over single people. The jury that voted to kill Socrates had 400 members. No wonder, later, Aristotle fled Athens.

In scary empire settings, teaching institutions tend to glide along with the system. A citizen dissents with little confidence if it's a nation which exports its enemies to be tortured in other countries.

Wordsworth knew the effect of civic fear. He had lived through the terrors of 1795 when the British powers-that-be used hideous methods to put down the new democratic idea of a man's having rights that the nobility cannot take away. This was the year in which working class British families were

---

[11] In the spring of 2003 The University of Minnesota's Carlson School of Management put on a conference on ethics called Moral Imagination. Surprisingly, much of the talk was of law rather than ethics and there was even talk of skirting the law and staying out of jail.

[12] In *The Republic*, II, first Thracymachus, then Glaucon, insist to Socrates that the only thing that *works*—actually works—for a fellow's career in human society is to appear to be just but in fact to be unjust. Rereading Plato's record of these conversations is a curious experience these days: one sees fast as lightning how teaching people to work the system is psychologically opposite to teaching people to have ideals and expend themselves to serve them—perhaps not unto death—but still, not to teach the young to serve the cynical and violent system.

reading aloud to one another Thomas Paine's *Rights of Man*. By 1799 Pitt had stopped the conversation about a man's having natural rights.

Our advice is to read the two extraordinary paragraphs of Wordsworth bearing in mind that a citizen was not safe from the British government. This isn't how people usually think of Wordsworth's famous "Preface," but how they usually think of it, and teach it, hasn't been very respectful of independence of mind, either.

One kind of toxic effect specific to manuscript workshopping is that if members of the workshop are coarse and given to amused scorn for philosophical caring, then any "tranquil connection-making between idea and sense-impression," as Wordsworth called it, or "re-entry" as Gerald M Edelman and Antonio Damasio call it, might draw amused or outright scornful grins from them. It is scary enough, in the ordinary creative-writing program, to get up your nerve and "put a manuscript up for workshopping." Why expose oneself to scorn? Why, too, give out numinous or mysterious plots or symbols or statements that no one else in the class seems to have written about?

No matter how well educated, no one—no one—wants to be thought a fool. No one wants to be publicly treated like one. A joke among German Intelligence agents in World War I was that the British would probably win the war because their agents didn't mind being thought fools, whereas no German could bear it.

Saving face is a huge dynamic. One needn't save face if one is consulting with one's own soul, so to speak. One does run the chance of being unwittingly crazy rather than original, but at least one needn't save face. If one is showing creative work to a teacher the teacher may insult it. One feels insulted. But feeling insulted is not a tenth the pain of losing face in a group. The moment we put a little kid into a "small group" to do creative writing together, his or her first care is to save face. We deceive ourselves if we don't grasp that. Well, maybe—an optimist might decide—no one in their small group is "coarse" or "cynical" and the child is in what school social workers call "a safe place."

A reality check: what random group of *H. sapiens* has ever been formed that hadn't one or two thugs or cynics or emotionally damaged people in it? And second, if little kids are psychologically "safe" in random classroom groups, why is it that school social workers *never ever* convene groups to do personal work together that are not "intentional"—that is, carefully screened by the worker in the first place, and thereafter constantly attended and steered by that social worker?

American adults may get to be 30 or 40 or even 50 before trusting any of their own finest feelings.

Harm Specific to Children Done by Putting Them into Small Creative-Writing Groups

Children are tremendously afraid of not being acceptable to one another. When we put them in "small groups," they are afraid not only of sounding ridiculous but of sounding one-tenth of a decibel different from anyone else, which is to say *original* at all. They will write the assigned pieces and read them aloud to the group or whatever is asked of them. But they will use center-bell-curve language and many *uh's* and *like's* as they dare begin with and end with so that they sound unpretentious and incompetent in a thoroughly unsnobbish way. If there is so much as *one* "kidder" in the group they will write jocularly. Thus they will make sure to exercise over and over *only* the kidding, sociable pathways in their heads. The worst of it is still worse, however: each minute they are seeing and hearing kidding and jocularity as *the proper norm*. They are practicing writing *for audience.* You can't serve two masters. If you are writing for audience you are not writing your own heart's truth.[13]

The commercial goal of anything, not just business but the arts, is now so normalized even to children that the headmaster of a conscientious and imaginative Eastern independent school wrote in its newsletter that the school was now teaching creative writing, using the workshop format. The children would hear one another's opinions of their compositions. He ended his letter with "…For what other reason would we write than to have an audience?"—a remark intended to be jocular and truthful.

We wrote to object, on psychological grounds.

The Head's reply was handy and jaunty. He wound up with "…besides, the children love it." Children love Snickers bars, too, but we don't give them a diet of false calories and concentrated sweetness—no matter how much they love it.

The Loft, a large and mainly excellent writers' educational and support organization in Minneapolis, advises its teachers "to help the students have fun with their writing."

Having fun with things means playing around with them. It is the opposite of deeply humorous literature, oddly enough. Huckleberry Hound, one of the earliest of a long half-century of Saturday leering and fun-making cartoons for children, was fun. *Huckleberry Finn* is art. Kidding, that effervescent mix of good humor and put-downs, became with Huckleberry Hound and other USA television the accepted children's kibble of wit. Whenever kidding becomes the model, earnestness and idealism are licked. Kidding and irony, not idealism, were the intellectual feed of American children who were allowed to watch Saturday morning cartoons.

Normalizing a kidding personality unfortunately disnormalizes an earnest, inquiring personality. Kidders get

---

[13] See Peter Elbow in footnote # 10

positive reinforcement (to use the beastly but accurate jargon of behaviorists), and earnest, idealistic children get negative reinforcement. They lose confidence in their own deeper feelings. At least, they lose confidence in mentioning them aloud.

This is especially true for American children, who are in groups most of the time from infant play dates to day-care to schools. They are wildly over-socialized. Over-socialized, not under, as children likely were on the Midwestern plains in the 1950s, even the 1970s.

Present-day children know how to be ironical about someone else's work while appearing merely to be mature—for "mature" read "of good humor." Group-socialized people tend to put a huge value on "having a ready sense of humor." It is vital to realize that considering light humor as a mark of maturity is a *business* value, not an *artistic*, not a *literary* value. One can't run a boardroom or an executive task force or even the poker-playing lunch breaks of an auto-assembly line unless one can do light jokes and keep them coming, too. Anecdotes should be short but importantly and preferably *scattershot*. They must not psychologically connect up in any noticeable way because they might suggest an underlying philosophy in the speaker. An underlying philosophy might suggest someone who might, if he or she kept on in that vein, become an evaluator who might in turn become a whistleblower.

Psychological Harm Done Youth by Middle- and High-School Workshopping Groups

Public schools and even the independent schools are setting ever younger people into little groups to work on one another's writing. Schools are doing this, although there isn't a stage-development theory in the world that doesn't point out dismaying effects of peer opinion on adolescents.

Along with their growing bodies, adolescents have ever-intensifying competitive feelings. Unless taught constraint, constraint, constraint, they will allow themselves various primitive practices of *H.sapiens*. A notable set of them involve the group-against-a-chosen-individual— bullying of one individual by the group; ostracizing of one person by the group, whether physically, as in middle- and late-stone age cultures, or using formal civic voting to ostracize as in classical Athens, or psychologically, as British public schools are so famous for doing. *Lord of the Flies* had it right: you take the boys out of the choir and away from the choirmaster (or adult mentorship of any kind) and they turn salacious and primitive.

American slang provides the perfect word to sling at the cruelty of ostracism. The word is *retro*. One is acting retro when, presumably too free of serious, principled leadership, one gives in to the natural inclination of mammals to disrespect originality or difference.

Bullying by adolescents of one another, especially when these adolescents are encouraged to comment on one another's writing, is frequently exquisite. Mammals have a predilection for sadism anyway. If we haven't been taught to constrain that sadism, we slip into savoring it. C.S. Lewis, a genuine, idealistic theologian, was nonetheless known, in his middle age, for having got together with his Inklings friends, who laughed and laughed when a new man in their group was stung by the exploding cigar that these grown men, university greats, had handed him.

Suppression of the Imagination Aggravated by the Workshopping of Manuscripts

We won't belabor this because the logic is not difficult: if people have to listen to other students' half- or fourth-educated remarks for hours and hours, they are *not* hearing the voice of experience in literature. They are not acquiring what we might call psychological taste—that is, the enjoyment of connecting small psychological dynamics that literature or life bring to us in fragments—connecting them into our own reflective, contemplative philosophy of things—our own general point of view.

The idea of "acquired philosophical taste" has a poor chance at currency in a culture most of whose young people no longer read any philosophy. We make a point of this because one way in which the workshopping of manuscripts blunts one's scholarship is that it takes up so much time. One can't look up other people who have thought in the past something like what we, this minute, listening to this new poem or story or even just this lecture, are thinking. Most MFA students have no expectation of being asked to look up connectives. Especially sad, because metaphors are the connectives for the reason that feeling any small band of fire run from work here at hand to feeling that is not here at hand is one of the essential ways for our species to enjoy *meaning* in life.

Graduate writing-class students complain that courses come with intriguing titles, but the syllabi fail to become reality. The time is spent in workshopping manuscripts. These student writers do learn a few minimal, usually technological points: Show, don't tell. Give particulars. Do not use dialogue for extended exposition. Pay attention to form. Keep a firm rein on point of view switches. They are good the way facts about the beam strengths of various stone and brick are good for people to know who plan to build cathedrals.

It is horrible, but not surprising, that so many writers' workshops denounce discussions of the *content* of literature as nonprofessional. An immediate disagreeable result of this is that so many manuscripts written in the United States have *no range of connectiveness* in their content. The United States has a foreign policy that affects millions of people in very striking ways. Surely more writers in their thirties have some feelings about their country and the unseen people affected by it? Or, on the other hand, you would think they must fee! some explosions of praise in their hearts for courage shown by others, outside their own lives? Is it going to be, they surely ask themselves, me talking all the rest of my writing life—more decades!—about my parents or my disability? What made the fiery light of Tolstoi's own life jump, through his writing, to other Russians? To Frenchmen? To passionate women?

Presumably, no one wasted his time in rubble. Like Virginia Woolf Tolstoi had hours of reading the best, learning languages spoken by *others*, not his family. But we are only guessing. The only useful way, I think, to look at this problem of workshopping and this literary problem of narcissism, is to ask ourselves: what obstructions did Tolstoi *not* have to bear? What disables the human mind from making flying connections?

The Practice of Workshopping Manuscripts Seen as an Environment Toxic to Re-entry in the Neocortex Because Workshopping Obviates Empathic Inquiry

As of the beginning of 2006, faculty members of MFA programs feel little curiosity about neuroscience. They make little or nothing of the amazing core consciousness of our species, with its behavior of messaging back and forth from neurons in one neighborhood not only to neurons of the next neighborhood but to neighborhoods situated here and there far away in the brain. This is like the difference between communities and networking.[14] In communities news spreads

---

[14] We are using the classical meaning of networking—relating to people connected to other people by mutual ideas—as opposed to the current usage, which is working the crowd.

gradually among neighboring people. In networking, some sort of invisible value or feeling takes flight and connects thinkers here with thinkers far away who have no practical propinquity at all. Startling new information from the outside—which in our neocortex means from the sense centers such as the visual centers at the back of the head—flies by chemo-electric firing to old neuronal neighborhoods where we have stored some previous opinion. The old previous opinions get reevaluated. The startling new perceptions get modified.

Peculiar to the human brain, neurologists now confidently say, is its behavior of *watching itself*. No other mammal appears to do that, even those mammals very close to us whose feeling and emotion circuitry is close to ours in some respects. Of course, like most animals, we use our brains to promote our own safety and our nourishment and our comfort and our seeking. Rats do as much. While we live along, however, *we watch ourselves living along* and we try to *refine and complicate our thinking*. We have a taste for refined thought.

The drawback of such self-observation is that we can't help noticing, during our self-contemplation, that we each must die. Enough to make anyone neurotic indeed. But human beings respond to that knowledge of death ahead in a number of ways. The one that concerns us in this book is how we at once maintain our mix of excitement about life and ourselves and do not deny our so evident fate. That is the business of art.

A propos, then, let's return to the Yeats poem and regard another side of it: the old man must die but his soul should meet that irreversible fate by singing, and then singing louder.

The false conventional wisdom of English departments is that the hard sciences tend to be reductive. Perhaps that was formerly true. It isn't true now.

If your schooling and college years and writers' conference-attending have given you what the Loft calls the "fun aspect of writing" —camaraderie and casual critiques, so that you have never learnt how to receive or yourself do empathic questioning as an elegant way of getting to your own *deepest* takes on things, you will not believe in the goal of empathy. You won't feel the loss of it. You may even never have heard of it. Empathy is not just a college-degree-level word for sympathy.

Empathic inquiry is a questioning process for finding out what else, near by, in your thinking is still unwritten but slightly touched on by a draft you have already written.[15]

It might be a wise, tough move to realize that you are learning to write in an at least partially toxic work environment. Reading how other people have noticed the stress of trying to fulfill private, comparatively idealistic goals, in the constant presence of work colleagues whose discussions take place on a totally different plane can be encouraging. William L. White has a marvelous chapter in an interesting work on corporate life that is especially applicable to thousands of writers' workshops.[16]

In a commercially-minded culture, good communication skills are taken to be ready humor and a glancing tolerance in group conversations. A low-key, sensible tone is seen as emotional maturity. And as for choice of subject to be handled in a mild, low-key tone, those who talk about external data are more respected than those who talk about moral and aesthetic feeling. We prefer the quiet emotion-less reports from satellite crews in outer space to raised voices about great invisible subjects. When you hear someone saying how sorry he or she is that the discussion escalated into raised voices and strong feelings, you are hearing the great trust that practical, commercially-minded people have for low-resolution comment.

---

[15] See Empathic Inquiry for Writers Only in the Appendix
[16] William L. White, *The Incestuous Workplace: Stress and Distress in the Organizational Family*. Center City, Minnesota 55012-0176 © 1986, 1997. 1-800-328-0094. Chapter 12, "Surviving Toxic Systems," starting on page 196.

Why any objection?

The objection is that great feelings inside a writer have a hard enough time recommending themselves at best. Perhaps that writer, what's more, has been taught that the beautiful lowing of the herd—a sound of many, a sound heard before, a sound that asks no cow in the herd to feel much of anything—that writer will have the dickens of a time to express anything intense. For example, to make a metaphor of any kind.

You may not trust that there is any greatness inside you. You may therefore have not the least curiosity to learn *why* a metaphor is so deep? You may have simply been told some technology about metaphors. A writing teacher, in fact, may have told you that metaphor is a wonderful *literary device*. He or she will be right, too. A metaphor is a literary device, but a literary device only in the sense that a Boeing 898 is rolling stock. You can drive it all over the tarmac at any airport. It steers, it goes fast, it brakes.

Here is what metaphors really are. They are a neurological stroke of genius: metaphors connect consciousness of one *kind* of thing or idea or feeling to another, *not identical* kind of thing or idea or feeling. And what is the good of that? Both things are lighted for a thousandth of a second by the connection. It is the contrast between the two things or the two ideas or the two feelings that anneals for us a totally new meaning. The force of the old man's being a tattered coat upon a stick is that people and sticks are not alike. Somehow the brain whipped across from the one to the other, though, and because of it we readers feel not Yeats's force of feeling but his force of *meaningfulness*, even about old age.

You can't do that kind of neurological wonder if you are workshopping manuscripts.

A Very Small Bibliography to Introduce People to some Up-to-Date Neurological Thinking

Damasio, Antonio. *The Feeling of What Happens: Body and Emotion in the Making of Consciousness.* New York: Harcourt, Inc. 1999.

Of the many fascinating machinations of the human brain discussed in this book, one of the most vital for writers is the sharp distinction Dr Damasio makes between raw emotion brought by perception and our bodies to us and the *feelings* which our brains draw from a mix of perceptions and inner neuronal work in the cortex.

Damasio, Antonio. *Looking for Spinoza: Joy, Sorrow, and the Feeling Brain.* New York: Harcourt, Inc. 2003.

As soon as we begin even *im passim* to study how our 100% biological brains work, we are struck by this amazing question: why does the brain of H.sapiens, if not abused and if educated to ideas at all, seem to work toward ethicality? It does. This cannot be discounted as leftover snags of Edwardianism.

Edelman, Gerald. *Wider Than the Sky: The Phenomenal Gift of Consciousness.* New Haven: Yale University Press, 2004.

This is the lovelier, more accessible of the two Edelman titles mentioned here. It is less throughgoing, however, since its purpose is different from that of *Bright Air, Brilliant Fire*, listed below.

Edelman, Gerald. *Bright Air, Brilliant Fire: On the Matter of the Mind.* New York: Basic Books, 1992.

Bright Air, Brilliant Fire takes the lay-reader through the serious revolution in neurological thinking of the latter quarter of the 20th century: that is, it explains the ingenious human brain as our evolved, 100% biological attribute. It dispatches dozens of quarrelsome and now out-dated theories. Further, for those of us who are lay-people, this book is informative about brain scholarship as well as current understandings of how this core part of us makes us what we are. NB: a charming aspect of both Damasio and Edelman is their appreciative acquaintance with the field of literature. It seems bizarre that literary people remain complacently ignorant of their work.

LeDoux, Joseph, *Synaptic Self: How our Brains Become Who We Are*. New York: Viking-Penguin, 2002

    LeDoux's discussion of how the various systems in our unmistakably multi-system brain connect or don't connect, overlap or don't overlap, converge to increase certain feelings or converge to tone down certain feelings, is fascinating: this author is a very welcoming teacher on the subject of how synapses, the mouth-pieces of our neurons, tell us our own story. Of course all brain science is scary for lay-readers, but LeDoux makes us more curious and more interested and more hopeful than scared.

A General Bibliography

Bly, Carol. *Beyond the Writers' Workshop: New Ways to Write Creative Nonfiction.* New York: Anchor Books, 2001.
Discussion of peer reviewing appears on pages 178-179; 151, 155-157; 15, 16; 23; and 41-43.

Freed, Lynn. *Reading, Writing, and Leaving Home: Life on the Page.* New York: Harcourt, Inc, 2005.
In "Doing Time" (p 135-174) Freed describes her struggles as a teacher of creative writing and the obstacles for students including the dangerous practice of workshopping. She says "the best I can do as a teacher is to function as a good editor, to help a student train his ear so that he can come to edit himself. That unless the student plans to spend his life moving from workshop to workshop, he will need to be able to rely on his own ear. And that if he does move from workshop to workshop, he is doomed to lose his sense of hearing anyway."

Janis, Irving L. *Groupthink: Psychological Studies of Policy Decisions and Fiascoes,* 2nd Edition. Boston: Houghton Mifflin, 1983.
Janis's book is the classic manual on how ad hoc task groups easily become toxic to the morality and intellectual elegance of their members.

Oliver, Mary. *A Poetry Handbook: A Prose Guide to Understanding & Writing Poetry.* New York: Harcourt, Brace Company, 1994.
Oliver says that, hands down, poetry cannot and will not be written except in solitude.

Phillips Exeter Academy, The Harkness Method. "Harkness tables."
Edward Harkness presented Exeter and other boarding schools with money for what has become known as "Harkness tables" in independent secondary schools. Harkness wanted 12 or so students to sit so they could see one another's faces and join common discussion. The Harkness method has proved wonderful in schools where it is tried. Our stance is that such collegial learning and thinking aloud is marvelous for history and the sciences, but detrimental to the artistic work of writing literature.

Schneider, Pat. *Writing Alone and with Others*, with a Foreword by Peter Elbow. New York: Oxford University Press, 2003. Here is the opposition to *Against Workshopping Manuscripts*. Schneider's intelligent book has much to say in favor of peer reviewing of manuscripts, and of writers helping one another in groups. The book is blessed in its Foreword by a first-rate writing teacher of the 20th century, Peter Elbow. Elbow made a concerted pedagogical war against authoritarianism in teaching. He also militated against all writing "for audience," a practice dear to most MFA programs today. Recommended: Elbow's essay called "Closing My Eyes As I Speak: An Argument for Ignoring Audience," in *College English* 49, no. 1 (January 1987): 50.

Ueland, Brenda, *If You Want to Write*. [First published by G.P. Putnam's Sons in 1938], reissued by Graywolf Press in 1987.

Ueland's teaching genius took several forms, but constantly weaving through her ideas is her insistence that artistic technique cannot be taught or learnt separately from learning to free up the writer's personal passions. This is an idea made little of in 2006 USA writing programs because you can't teach people personal passion in a group whose intelligence and levels of compassion and, most disheartening of all, levels of ability to concentrate on anything intense vary too much to count on. For all the talk about being "safe" in a writers' workshop, most MFA workshops are socially in compliance but spiritually not safe.

White, William L, *The Incestuous Workplace: Stress and Distress in the Organizational Family*. Center City, MN 55012-0176, 800-328-0094. This was first published by Lighthouse Training Institute, in 1986. Hazelden Press republished it in 1997.

Please see especially the chapter called "Surviving Toxic Systems," 196f. If workshopping manuscripts is indeed a procedure toxic to serious originality, then White's suggestions for psychological survival are invaluable to MFA and summer conference writers.

Great Literature for Writers

Why read the greats?

If a carpenter has never seen a mortice and tenon, he or she may never realize how wonderfully serious joins can be made in lumber. If a writer has never read great literature, he or she may never realize the wonderfully serious connections that can be made in one's own mind.

Short Stories

"Bliss," Katharine Mansfield
"The Undeclared Major," Will Weaver
"Birthday Cake," Raymond Carver
"Rikki Tikki Tavvy," Rudyard Kipling
"Mademoiselle Fifi," Guy de Maupassant
"The Short Happy Life of Francis Macomber," Ernest Hemingway
"Royal Beatings," Alice Munro
"Gooseberries," Anton Chekhov
"The Dead," James Joyce
"How Much Land Does a Man Need?" Leo Tolstoi
"What Men Live By," Leo Tolstoi
"The Enormous Radio," John Cheever
"The Kugelmass Episode," Woody Allen
"The Rocking-Horse Winner," D.H. Lawrence
"The Lottery," Shirley Jackson
"Guests of the Nation," Frank O'Hara
"The War Prayer," Mark Twain
"For Esme with Love and Squalor," J.D. Salinger
"Battle Royal" Ralph Ellison
"Gryphon," Charles Baxter
"The Tender Organizations," Carol Bly

Novels

Anna Karenina, Leo Tolstoi
Buddenbrooks, Thomas Mann
Catcher in the Rye, J.D. Salinger
The Liberty Campaign, Jonathan Dee
Remains of the Day, Kazuo Ishiguro
Sons and Lovers, D.H. Lawrence
Emma, Jane Austen
Little Women, Louisa May Alcott
Native Son, Richard Wright

Novellas

The Woman Lit by Fireflies, Jim Harrison
A Simple Heart, Gustave Flaubert
A Mother's Tale, James Agee
Youth, Joseph Conrad
The Death of Ivan Illich, Leo Tolstoi
A Christmas Carol, Charles Dickens

Essays

A Room of One's Own, Virginia Woolf
"I Was Really Very Hungry," M.F.K. Fisher
"How to Cut the Throat Properly" Brenda Ueland
Teaching a Stone to Speak, Annie Dillard

Poems

"Wild Geese," Mary Oliver
"Poem in Three Parts," Robert Bly
"Like Loving Chekhov," Denise Levertov
"Musée des Beaux Arts," W.H. Auden
"Wasteland," T.S. Eliot
"Birches," Robert Frost

"The Mind is Wider Than the Sky," Emily Dickinson
"Sailing to Byzantium," W.B. Yeats
"Alarm," John Rezmerski
"The World is Too Much With Us," William Wordsworth
"Loveliest of Trees," A.E. Housman
"The Sea Eats What it Pleases," Bill Holm

Plays

The later plays only, William Shakespeare

William Wordsworth
Preface to the *Lyrical Ballads*, 2nd Edition, 1801.

We reproduce below 2 passages showing this poet's amazing prescience. Two centuries before any neuroscientists had begun noticing and *attempting to measure, and thus predict from, neuron activity in the neo cortex*, Wordsworth describes re-entry. Incidentally, it is the comfortable habit of middle-brow hard-science people to jeer at "anecdotal" insights. Imaginative literature is mainly anecdotal. The pejorative use of the word "anecdotal" should be seen as intellectually out of date. If anecdotal means something to disrespect, how come one of the world's leading anecdotal poets was 197 years ahead of his time in grasping re-entry?

1. "For all good poetry is the spontaneous overflow of powerful feelings: and though this be true, poems to which any value can be attached were never produced on any variety of subjects but by a man who, being possessed of more than usual organic sensibility, had also thought long and deeply. For our continued influxes of feeling are modified and directed by our thoughts, which are indeed the representatives of all our past feelings and, as by contemplating the relation of these general representatives to each other, we discover what is really important…"

2. "For the human mind is capable of being excited without the application of gross and violent stimulants; and he must have a very faint perception of its beauty and dignity who does not know this, and who does not further know that one being is elevated above another in proportion as he possesses this capability. It has therefore appeared to me that to endeavor to produce or enlarge this capability is one of the best services in which, at any period, a writer can be engaged; but this service, excellent at all times, is especially so at the present day. For a multitude of causes

unknown to former times, are now acting with a combined force to blunt the discriminating powers of the mind, and, unfitting it for all voluntary exertion, to reduce it to a state of almost savage torpor. The most effective of these causes are the great national events which are daily taking place, and the increasing accumulation of men in cities, where the uniformity of their occupations produces a craving for extraordinary incident, which the rapid communication of intelligence hourly gratifies... I think upon this degrading thirst after outrageous stimulation..."

Empathic Inquiry for Writers Only[1]

Empathic inquiry has two promising instruments for creative writers. First, it helps authors to become aware of their own opinions as either majority notions in their brains or as surprisingly contradictory (minority) opinions in their brains. Second, it leads authors to asking questions about feelings of characters in stories not yet realized.

All empathic inquiry naturally is the second stage of writing any manuscript. The first stage is one's conscious determination to write this manuscript, whatever it is. One may do it out of lunging glorious inspiration, or one may do it doggedly like someone lost on a desert island making a record lest all be lost. In any case, before practicing empathy, we write something that is going to be a piece of writing of some sort.

Then we look at it, now determined to go deeper with it. This means keeping other people out of it. It means we will question the manuscript ourselves.

This empathic inquiry for writers offers four steps:

1. You make up your mind to a psychological truth that most people have never heard and (as they tell therapists if they know one or two) they certainly aren't going to swallow whatever else they swallow: that you have contradictory ideas in your head. All are genuinely yours. There isn't just one true "self" on any issue: there are several. If this idea seems odd see the list of neuroscience books in the appendix—and second, bear in mind how many times people say "I'm of two minds about it" and "I go back and forth about that." Reading even a very little neuroscience will build authors' confidence in their own minority opinions.

---

[1] For an all-purpose empathy-inquiry format please see pp 49-50 in *Beyond the Writers' Workshop: New Ways to Write Creative Nonfiction* (Anchor Books), 2001

2. If you are writing an essay, you ask yourself these questions:

   a. Every argument has three aspects to it: the original data it is based on, the feelings it generated at the time, and the meaning I decided it had then, and, as I look back on it, now. Data, feelings, meaning. That means having a true, non-lying anecdote for each idea.
   b. Is everything I have argued for really true? Apart from the question of lying about data—absolutely apart from that![2] —I said certain events or feelings meant such-and-such. But in fact, is that not true? Our own minds are deeper and more truthful than most received junk opinions from the culture. Unfortunately, what we hear bruited around by others has megaphone strength compared with the shy minority feelings inside ourselves.

3. If you are writing fiction ask each character on the list of your characters as many questions as you can: what are they about? How did this situation you've put them in strike them? Where would they rather have been? —as many questions as you can.

4. Step 4 can be a painful realization. That is, the entire essay so far, or the entire story so far, or large chunks of either, may not be the most passionate subject in your head. You may have done pages and pages of writing in good faith. But now—but now—but now that you have spread it out in front of you, you see that what you *really care about* and want to write about is at least partially different.

---

[2] No essay, memoir, biography, or autobiography should have any *conscious* lying in it. Because memory has no one "site" in the brain but is a mix of various neuronal combinations, events won't be remembered in the same way by a given single person—never mind the differences in how two people recall one occasion. The idea is to ask yourself to tell what you best believe is true.

The best gift of empathic questioning is that we can deepen our first take on things. We're not stuck. Empathy is the *real* fire of what is so generally and tiresomely called "the writing process."

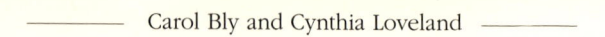

About the Authors

Carol Bly's most recent teaching is The Short Story in the Hamline University MFA program, fall semester, 2005. She will be teaching in June, 2006, at the University of Nebraska Annual Writers' Conference.

Her most recent books are *Beyond the Writers' Workshop* (Anchor Books, 2001), *My Lord Bag of Rice: New and Selected Stories* (Milkweed, 2000), and *Changing the Bully Who Rules the World* (Milkweed, 1996. 3rd printing 2005). 3 chapters of her unpublished novel, *Shelter Half,* have now appeared in *The Idaho Review* and *Prairie Schooner*. A short story will appear in *Prairie Schooner*, Spring 2006.

Carol Bly was an Edelstein-Keller Distinguished Author at the University of Minnesota and has received the Minnesota Humanities Commission's career award.

She and Cynthia Loveland are co-publishers of Bly & Loveland Press, www.blyandloveland.com. Bly & Loveland books include *A Shout to American Clergy,* 2005, *Stopping the Gallop to Empire,* 2004, and *Three Readings for Republicans and Democrats,* 2003.

Cynthia Loveland is retired from her career as a Social Worker. After earning her MSW at the University of Minnesota she worked for nine years in county social service in rural Minnesota. She then worked for almost 30 years as a School Social Worker for the St. Paul, Minnesota, Public Schools as practitioner and as Lead School Social Worker. She has been active in professional Social Work organizations including NASW (National Association of Social Workers) and MSSWA (Minnesota School Social Workers' Association.)